BOA EDITIONS LTD

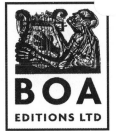

BUFFALO GIRL

BUFFALO GIRL

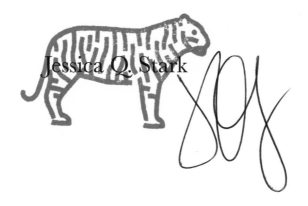

Jessica Q. Stark

AMERICAN POETS CONTINUUM SERIES, No. 199

BOA Editions, Ltd.   Rochester, NY   2023

First Edition
23 24 25 26 7 6 5 4 3 2 1

For information about permission to reuse any material from this book, please contact The Permissions
Company at www.permissionscompany.com or e-mail permdude@gmail.com.

Publications by BOA Editions, Ltd.—a not-for-profit corporation under section 501 (c) (3) of the United
States Internal Revenue Code—are made possible with funds from a variety of sources, including public
funds from the Literature Program of the National Endowment for the Arts; the New York State Council
on the Arts, a state agency; and the County of Monroe, NY. Private funding sources include the Max
and Marian Farash Charitable Foundation; the Mary S. Mulligan Charitable Trust; the Rochester
Area Community Foundation; the Ames-Amzalak Memorial Trust in memory of Henry Ames, Semon
Amzalak, and Dan Amzalak; the LGBT Fund of Greater Rochester; and contributions from many
individuals nationwide. See Colophon on page 126 for special individual acknowledgments.

Cover Design: Sandy Knight
Cover Art: Photograph courtesy of Kimle Mac Quick
Interior Design and Composition: Michelle Dashevsky
BOA Logo: Mirko

BOA Editions books are available electronically through BookShare, an online distributor offering
Large-Print, Braille, Multimedia Audio Book, and Dyslexic formats, as well as through e-readers that
feature text to speech capabilities.

Cataloging-in-Publication Data is available from the Library of Congress.

BOA Editions, Ltd.
250 North Goodman Street, Suite 306
Rochester, NY 14607
www.boaeditions.org
A. Poulin, Jr., Founder (1938–1996)

*"no one knows who one is and
the texture of knowing this
doesn't feel human."*

—Justin Phillip Reed, *Indecency*

CONTENTS

THREE

For the original Buffalo Girl, Mạc Lệ Kim,
and all Buffalo Girls thereafter

Against Knowing

for what's-his-name

Against naming, too
Against notion, ruling,
circumstantial love

Against symmetry—
its little string leading
back to the house

Against California's
exclusion of diacritics

Against emptying
nuance into mess

cu, cu, cu:
root, penis, old

tao, tao, tao:
apple, nonsense, create

Against creation of
an untrue gullet

Against truth and
reason's steady ruse

What brought you here?
Who did you want?
What moves you?

Against nonsense as
the stony lake

Against useful bodies
Against tonguing the wound
Against knowing what

keeps you still some nights,

what still keeps you up on others.

ONE

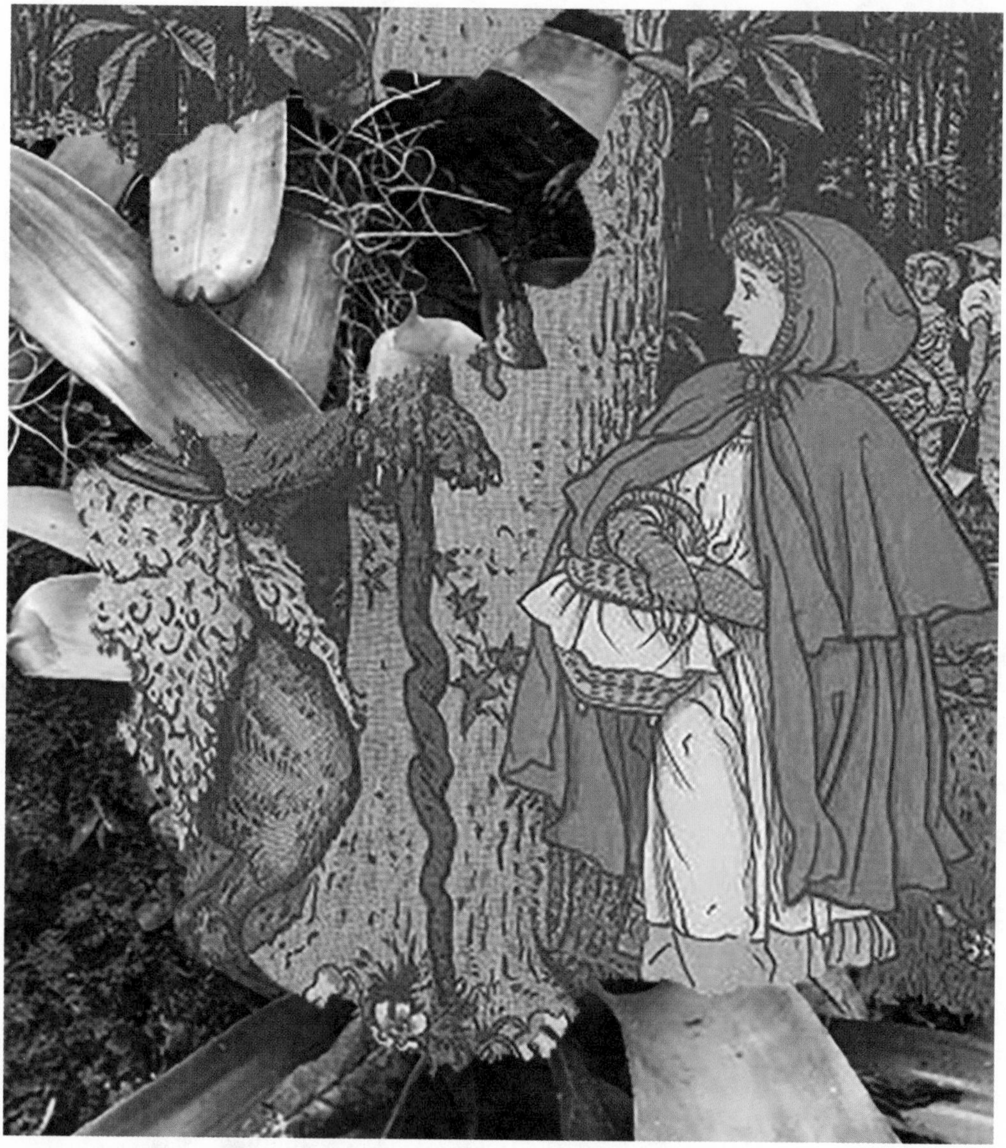

Phylogenetics

There was a lonely cabin,
Within a dark, old wood,

And in it, with her mother,
There dwell Red Riding Hood.

When it began isn't clear, but isn't it obvious that   we always had a knack
for stories about little girls in danger?

Nice girls, stupid girls, naughty girls, girls bleeding and   holding baskets
of wine: each knot another route to pity-blame the foal

Why not a hard-edge (for once)   let the girl wander where she pleases
For the moral of the story isn't always

the same, and how's the one go where   she doesn't die   alone and pretty?
Where no Huntsman comes around to cut   her out?

Who will answer   for the anonymous limb, taking?   Where once a wood, a
rice paddy. Where once a hole, a tooth.

Songs of the Buffalo Girl: wet   strands in a   basket housing   little
figures that know their way around in the dark

Look now to Little Red Cap, taking all of her known objects to bed,   taking
off her overcoat to reveal fine downy fur.

The Wild Water Buffalo

are both diurnal and nocturnal,
which may seem contradictory

unless my mother's whistling

into another life around the

kitchen island, the night sky
barely breaking into a new task.

Sleep is a luxury for the revealed,
small territories of the ever-on-

time, monolingual—monopoly

tenderfoots of land and soot.

Once on a sojourn from
responsibility I traveled

to my mother's country, drank
the water and fell ill for four days.

In the eternal break of my fever,

we hiked to a riverbed for a bath—
the sweet, cool slip on my skin.

I plunged into another view,

broke water, and met eyes with

a frightening mass, half-submerged
under our murky blanket.

Bathing with a beast is no burden.

And how many ways can
I break a mask? How many

syllables would it take to
travel from one's own stubborn

and beastly tongue?

The Old Man in the Tree

Let's begin before we are dead

she said her first
memory was a

school wrapped in morning

darkness

a story about

walking girls and time
that passed too slowly

and inside that time, in purple
light and twigs at sun-up, sat an

old man she knew waiting
for her in a   tree.

The first lesson
in fortitude against

invisible male members
is knowing one's   own

weight in wind and solitude
against

memory's   dead leaves.

The rustling laughter, she wanted,
the hands like gnarled root.

Passing by you might mistake
a star for feeble eyes, arranging

stones and price tags in
exchange for departure.

It's not cheap.

One morning in front of the
tree and the man of stars,

a white-cheeked monkey
bit her hard

and sat down to his meal
of fresh flesh.

These days she still thumbs
the scar (forearm, right-side)

when she's nervous around petty
men in power,

when she's writing
a sacrificial heart—a trivial thing

when you are so hungry.

Sharp, dull bang against
an evening in

Vietnam, 1975, when her leaves
began quietly turning in onto

themselves,

undoing heroes

and circumstance.

And the corpses
were   forgiven

their fantasies.

And the tree was
cut into   paper.

And the TV sets were left out for good.

In the street: just quiet,
like holding a breath

before the steady task of fate.

And an old man somewhere high

was feeling satisfied with
his meal and his lodging and

he sang:

Oh, Buffalo Girls,

won't you come
out tonight,

come out tonight,
come out tonight,

Oh, Buffalo Girls,

won't you come out tonight,

and dance by the
light of the moon?

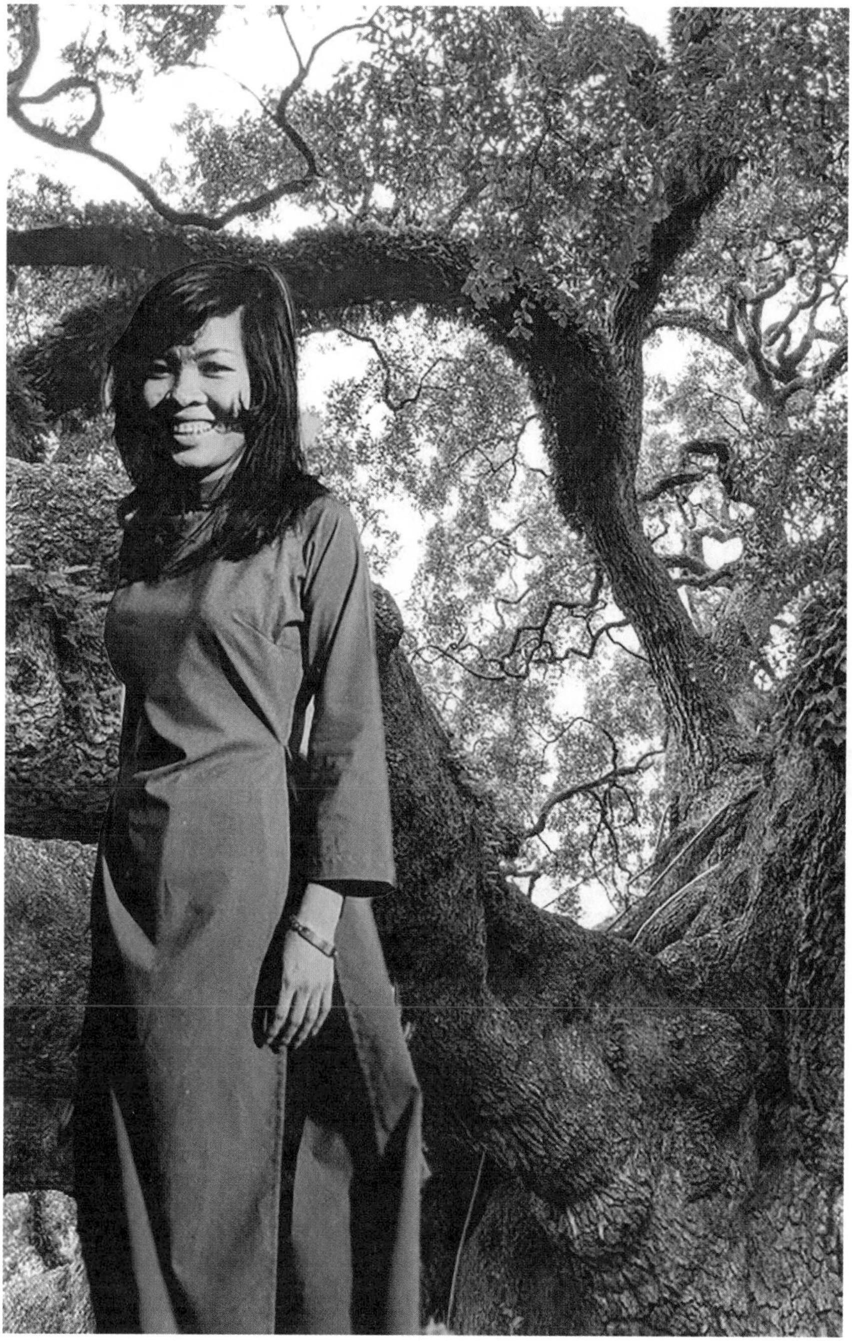

Little Red Riding Hood

after Charles Perrault

Moral: Children, especially attractive, well-bred young ladies, should never talk to strangers, for if they should do so, they may well provide dinner for a wolf.

Once upon a time in
the prettiest creature

Her mother fond
Her grandmother doted

This good woman

set to go to a village

through the wood
with a wolf and

a very great mind, with

woodcutters nearby—

tap, tap.

Who's there?

I say wolf, but there
are various kinds.

Impact Sport

By age 15 I was a hungry, red wolf.

I worked at JoAnn Fabrics one
summer—scowling women forming

lines at the back of my hangover and a
terrible crush that kept blooming over

patterns beneath my palms.

I scanned coupons and resisted knowing
the definition of a window valance. So

many sighs from women in search

of a texture, a measurement, some small
tool that I could never afford. After I
learned the cameras were decoys,

it was all over: stickers, hot-glue guns,
a bounty of expensive scissors I never used.

Most nights I brought sneakers and ran

the four miles back to my childhood home,
happy to be moving in the dark from white light.

It was worse than McDonald's, which in truth

was somewhat fun—working the butt of
every parent's joke in the '90s, living the
worst-case-scenario at 16. Kind of

punk rock the way MJ and I figured out
how to deliver unrecorded beverages
in the drive-thru and pocket the

complicated math. Though it was here

where I found the limitations of my face,
where the fry guy would hold me

by the shoulders in the walk-in freezer
and plant a greasy mouth on mine. And
what else could you do but laugh about it

later with MJ in the same freezer
sitting next to the chilled cookie dough
with a fistful of nuggets, each of you

taking too long of a break, taking
mouthfuls of soft serve and the feeling

that we could never truly die.

Fast-forward to college and I'm at the
campus bookstore, I'm at the library,
I'm cleaning professors' offices and

watching their sick cats. But worst of all
I'm telemarketing, which was an unknown

quantity of death, a bait-and-switch

operation for selling car listings
with a scripted, ghost's voice
through the phone. Later,

I'd be back alive and against
the clock trying to find a thrifted

shift that would everlast dancing

in New York City all night. The
origins of the phrase "go-go dancing"
derives from the French *a gogo*

meaning abundance, meaning galore,

which links to the word *la gogue*, or a
French word for joy. I don't know if

I ever found happiness, shaking my

ass over glass cups and faces going
gloss. But most nights in that

mechanical suture I felt like air,

maybe freer than a walk-in freezer,
my time and movement in abundance,

like no one could ever clock me in,

like no one ever could touch me again—
not my face, not my hand, not my teeth,

my, what big—
my, what sharp—

like I'd never eat that red hunger again.

Ballad of the Red Wisteria

Because of its hardiness and tendency to escape cultivation, these non-native wisterias are considered invasive species in many parts of the United States, especially the Southeast, due to their ability to overtake and choke out other native plant species.

Is red   love   with a knack
for breaking code   first memories:
sure, first   memories of home
include a   pick-pocket
or two,   a stolen newspaper
route   coupon drawers and
ketchup   packets: but that's *survival*, baby
she sed   like slick,
Neapolitan   ice sticks in summer
like   cool rockets   red
white and   blue   there is no antidote for
mixed   blood   there is no domicile
for   the invasive species   why
the fuck   would I garden   sed mama
in a *mood*   looking like John Wayne as
best you   can after last night's
over-the-   fence with the white
neighbors   about pool
parties   & sensor lights (again), heard
a word   stick like sweat, all pink-mouthed
rounded O   shot out like dandelions
sprouting   in the yard, like they
were there   the whole time saw
mama   furl inside like a thorn, sliding
the door on   things you don't mention
again, like   don't worry we'll steal their fucking
nectarines   I mean the good ones, trời ơi con,
she sed   it doesn't mean anything

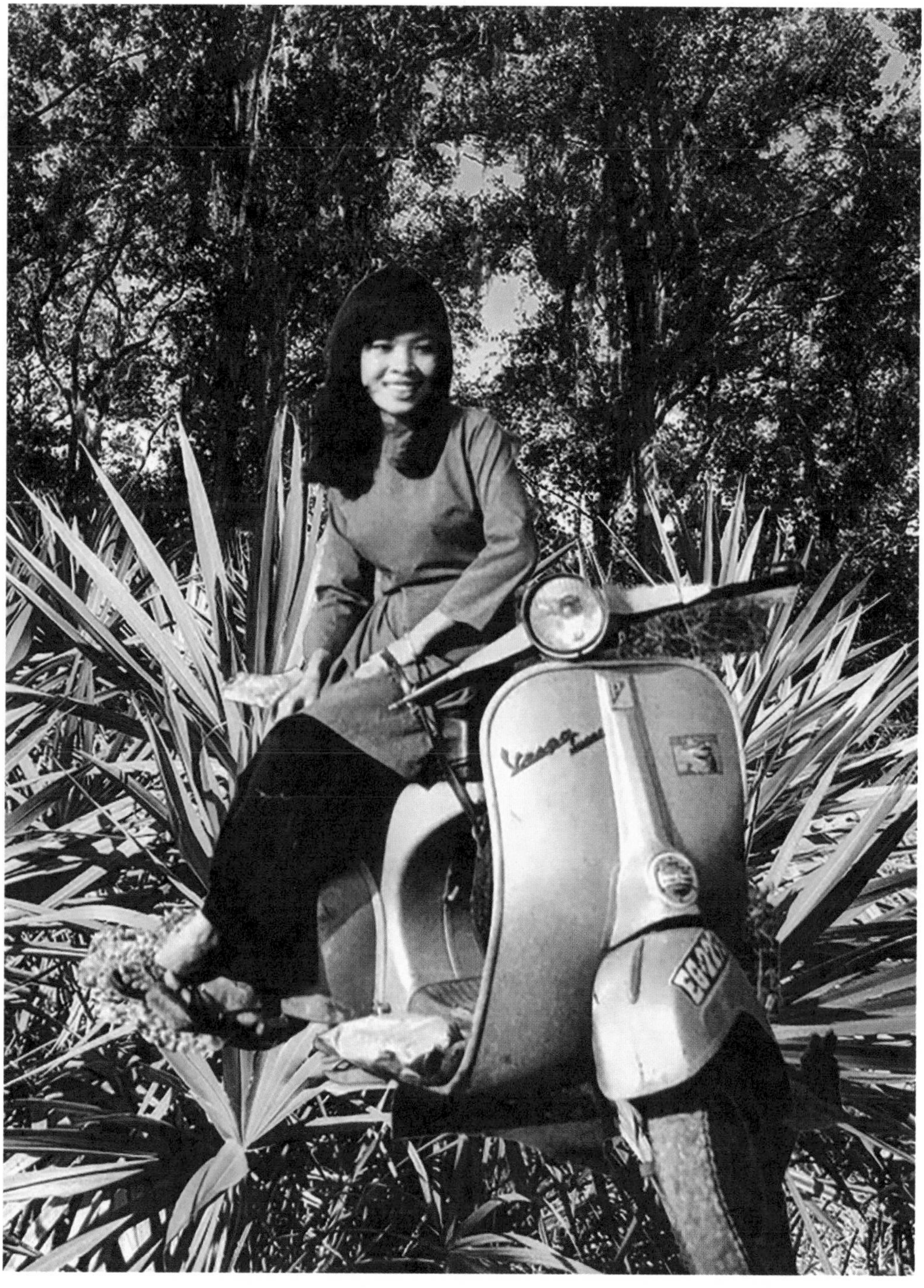

Little Red Riding Hood

after B. Wilmsen

For a while she kept to

      flowers, but
little girls like to eat.

      Sharp teeth on
      the edge of wood.

WHO'S THERE?

said the latch,
dark and rough.

In a timid tone she cried,

THE CHILD,

POINTED
AND WILD.

The Stony Lake

or the way I named my silver whip of a son   Bảo Đại
half-joke,   half-history,   my mother's
smile   curving around Vietnam's   wayward son—
hiding glamorously   in France   while   his
country   writhed   against a static sea,   a
romance to be so   unapologetically   rove, to
say nothing   of   poetic justice, or   the time
my white   grandfather   asked us children   why we
didn't   have our   father's blue eyes—   four
fawns   quietly   awaiting our meal of violence—
I was genuinely curious, too,   about biology
and   our place   in the matter   which felt
like a   hollow

          about   *mongoloid*:   a word

that   sounded like a   broken bird   in flight
so   terrible   and magnificent and   magnificent
today   is another   stony   lake and my   sister
cannot get out of bed   I am the mother to a   blue-
eyed child   this is not a metaphor   or any
other   consolation,   find   yourself an
itinerary for   undoing, Reader,   for   hiding   in
plain sight,   for impurity   rearing   its
unbleached   sightline   against shingle   *there*—
right at the base   *I said look*   right
at   the   foundation of your   first-born home

Little Red Riding Hood

after the Brothers Grimm

Half a league from the village
Little Red entered the wolf

what a wicked creature
to have something good

pretty flowers growing
deeper into the house

the wolf lifted the latch
without saying a word

she could carry no more

what big ears
what large hands

the wolf's skin

revived Little Red
to run into the wood
to guard her way

the house was a great stone

the child began to slip

The Light of the Moon

I danced with a gal with a hole in her stocking
And her knees was a-knockin' and her shoes was a-rockin'
I danced with a gal with a hole in her stocking
And we danced by the light of the moon

Years after the first wolf and the
discharge of painted visions,

Red sought another errand after

the collapse of her country's face.

What would she give, a mouth
asked, to secure safe passage?

Decorations on decoration.

They would empty the basket
in the light of the moon, and

Red would address the
lessons of a former silhouette:

if something must be taken

away, continually, one must

learn to cut out its value.

She would find another way
through the deep woods with

a set of plastic furs.

That night, she quietly
slipped the four-starred fish

away from its fate, would

muddy honors across flesh ::

tasting nothing, but soot and
and salt and unwashed hair.

Hungry Poem

It wasn't exactly like we were poor, but we were hungry
knock-off saltines, knock-off Cheez-its, knock-offs of knock-
offs going stale (eat them) on lined shelves what survival
textures into blood wouldn't be called grace or any
timid plume we were a fucking wolfpack
for a free sample, so *hungry hungry* for gorged a
belly without price-tags bits of bone in our
teeth and our hair one Spring my gums bled out
for two months straight the little cookies
punctuating each nervous ending and when I left when
I felt so gone I picked my own body's price (tradition)
(never simple) and danced it near-dead on a
stairwell underground I nearly tripped more
than once on a stranger's upturned eye that looked so
hungry *hungry,* that insistent invitation—
a little cabin in the woods— & I'd turn course
to pluck rove flowers, again & *again,* (silly girl)
everyone knows you can't write your own death
(I know) I've acquired hunger across modest lines
what would it cost you to watch me eat?

Hungry Poem

My mother prides herself on being a Good American
expresses anger when I dismiss myself for five years,

first to South Korea, then to Spain; *Korea is full of assholes*
she says—references a long layover and a fistful of

cashiers that hated her face like I hate my face; *you'll see*—
I didn't see, but I did come back, and I did come back to her strong

arm tracing around the kitchen island, a
secret in her pocket most of the time we aren't sick with

what wouldn't have been
there is a decrease in white

frontal brain matter in most diagnosed kleptomaniacs, meaning *what*—
meaning impulse control, meaning behavioral medicine for zippered jeans

white lilies popping up in every yard, blooming refuse to refuse
and how else should I assemble this particular brand of cruelty?

Most of my time is spent thinking up different scenarios that
aren't sensual, don't feel sensual, and in every other episode

I'm only here because of that stupid war—insert unknown relatives' faces
across the airplane's aisle, my head resting on someone else's backrest

pointing towards the Atlantic, pointed in any direction other than home

The Tale of the Tiger-Women

after Huan Chih-chun

Someone told me the
subject of tigers then

went to transform
herself.

Dark forest along
narrow path.

THE NIGHT IS LONG AND
    I BEAR THE HUNGER.

The girl said: I AM
HUNGRY, TOO.

There are a great many
dangers along   the

stretched rope. Moonlight
exposed the long gut, and

not the girl. It is still better
to be the tree than the

sleeping-mat, in truth. A

tiger afterwards was
    breaking a burden.

The woman leading tigers
pointed at   the tree

and said   there   a human

being deceived them.

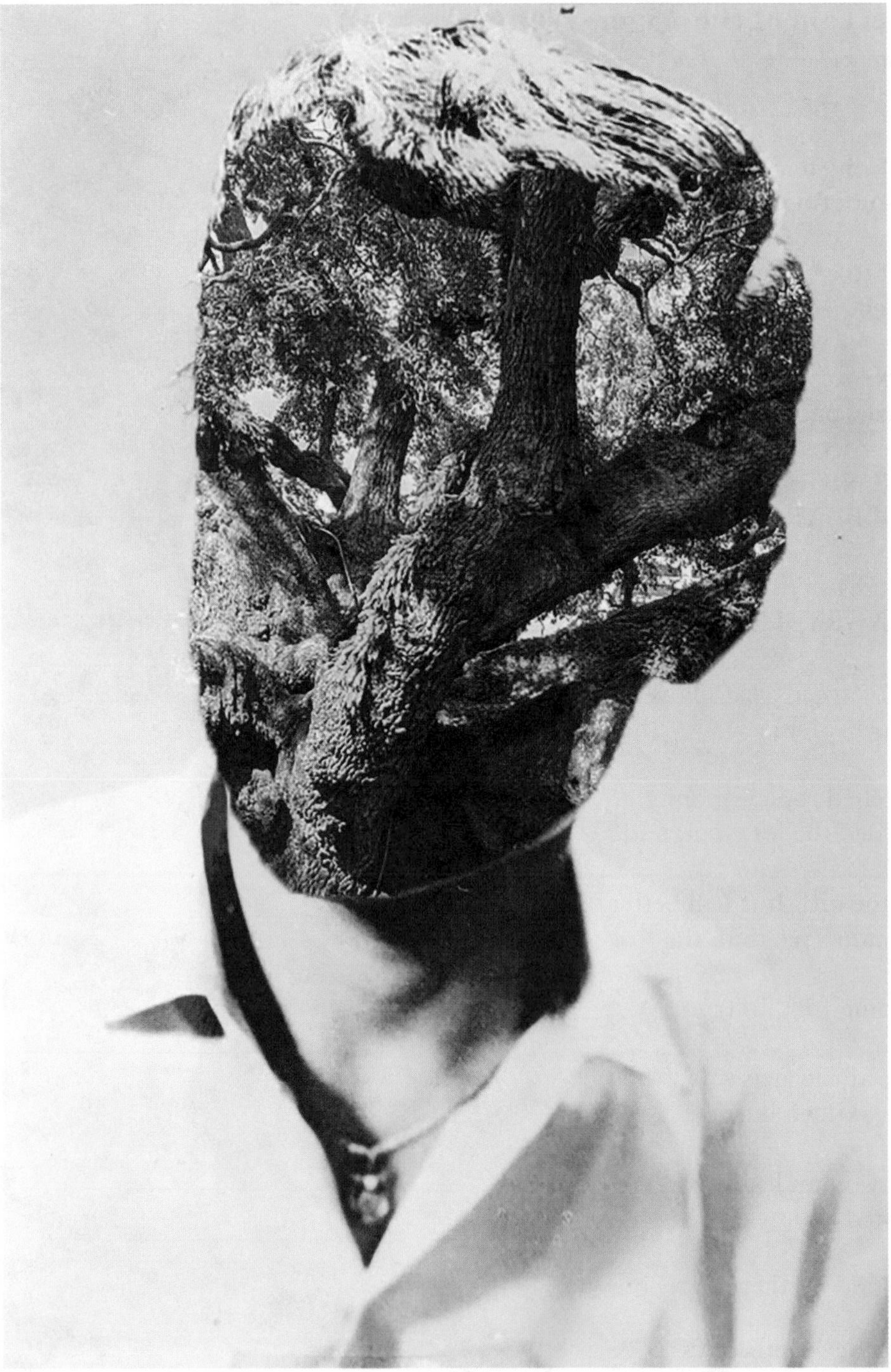

The One in Which the Wolf Wins

We cut you out of it,

the whole belly

giving way to red

determination.

On the bed, an apology

and a DNR note left for

tidy ends that

Red refused

to believe the cost

of cunning

an inheritance

of the deep woods

or that the price

of staying whole

means hunting the little

girl with the bread, the

one who wandered into

the world as a wonder

sharp little red who

loved a simple, beautiful

flower more than herself,

who trusted everything,

except her own nose and

eyes. To find her deeply

set into one's own basket:

your children, *your first-*

born child. The cost

to cut her out :: to

carry a rotting head

home to recall one's

place among the hunger,

among the dogtooth violets.

Con Cào Cào

You can paint a woman

      by the river   bank, but

     you can't ever imitate

  a sound, fully. This story is

not simple. Let me leave it

     to its own   devices: my

   desire—to rinse the rice without

measurement, to eat the fisheye

in   ecstasy, to sell my   tchockies,
     my face, to leave

each bound syllable

     there by the   bank,
beside the wounds of dead-less

soldiers   asking nothing,

     finding nothing   interesting

       about the woods
        or history's

          mincing   mixing

   rot   circumstance   love

foil   ocean   metal   salt   into air.

And everything   even absence

leaves a trace within   the body.

And everyone   even truth

          is their own   version of memory.

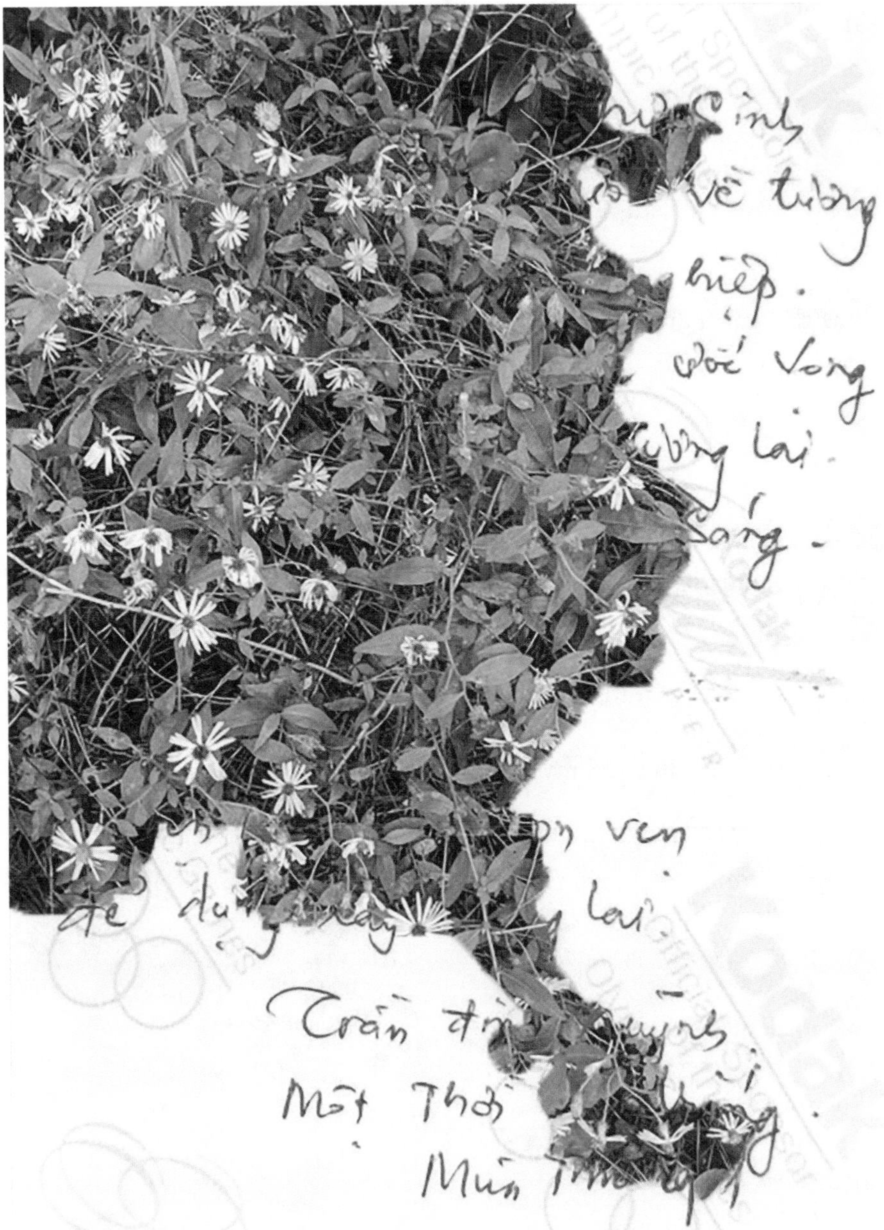
sinh
về tương
hiệp.
đổi vọng
tương lai.
sáng.
ven
để dựng xây
lại.
Trần đình
Một Thời
Mùa Thu

On Passing

For years I tried on different stories about my body

to use the body as a rinsing husk.

Language here is also a delicate peapod, a shell
that forms the world and its fantastic borders.

For years I ignored the sentence in my body.

Who came and who went—a blank ledger.

In this body is my mother's body
who paid the fantastic price in
fairy tales written mostly by men.

I have my mother's eyes and her teeth before they all fell out.

I have a rare ring size around my tongue and to some, this is monstrous.

She still speaks to me in Vietnamese, knowing that my
lessons stopped nine years ago, that nobody speaks it here.

But I can still say *how are you, happy birthday, I love you.*

This is a sufficient rind.

This is the only way I can say,

let's find a way out of here
let's take apart the woods

o

The discomfort I have with my whiteness resembles betrayal to the sentence in my body.

A short blade, an omission, a long tooth I can't extract.

The second conditional clause sets a resting stone at the head of this longwinded route.

If I drank the wine, I wouldn't sleep well,
so I never sleep.

My whiteness makes some people comfortable;
it provokes the most absurd confessions.

A lot of people would like to hold me still, *confess*.

Is there violence at the origin of each known word? I look up
hybrid and arrive again to my wakefulness; afraid.

The grammar of my body relies on certain conditionals.

o

If it had never—
If he hadn't asked—
If the war wasn't so—
If the body had refused—
If they hadn't—
If the first time wasn't so—
If there were fewer family members—
If she hadn't wanted—
If he hadn't fled—
If it wasn't so bad—
If the Americans weren't so—

If she could stay still.

o

My mother said when I was born, she was afraid.

Women born in the Year of the Tiger are fabled as
too much in their own story. They're risk-takers in

this world, which typically spells feminine ruin.

She laughs often at her small monster, leaping again into dark.

She was also afraid of the fourth scar;
they said she'd be ripped apart between white walls.

This country is not for the faint-hearted; I will wear it.

This is the sentence in my body, decorated.

I cannot (not) take it off.

o

I am here because my mother settled a debt.

There was a conditional in her body.

There was a conditional in her father's body in a body of water.

I am not frightened of risks,
but I am afraid of drowning.

I dreamed of it all year long before my son's first howl.

My mother told me to name him twice to keep away bad spirits.
I named him thrice and kept him low; tried to avoid his face.

The typo on his birth certificate says *gone*
and with this, you looked satisfied.

I paced around trying to figure out how to put him back in line.

All night long my bristles stood on fantastic ends.
I meant to weep but could only growl.

You said nothing and brought back Panera to celebrate.

Free coffee, a punchcard, meal vouchers
white like paper, like my powerful calves.

Hmmmmm, yagga, yagga. All tongue and tooth.

How jagged I felt those few weeks out—my story gone rogue.

How without language we might finally be vanished,
touchless, *free.*

TWO

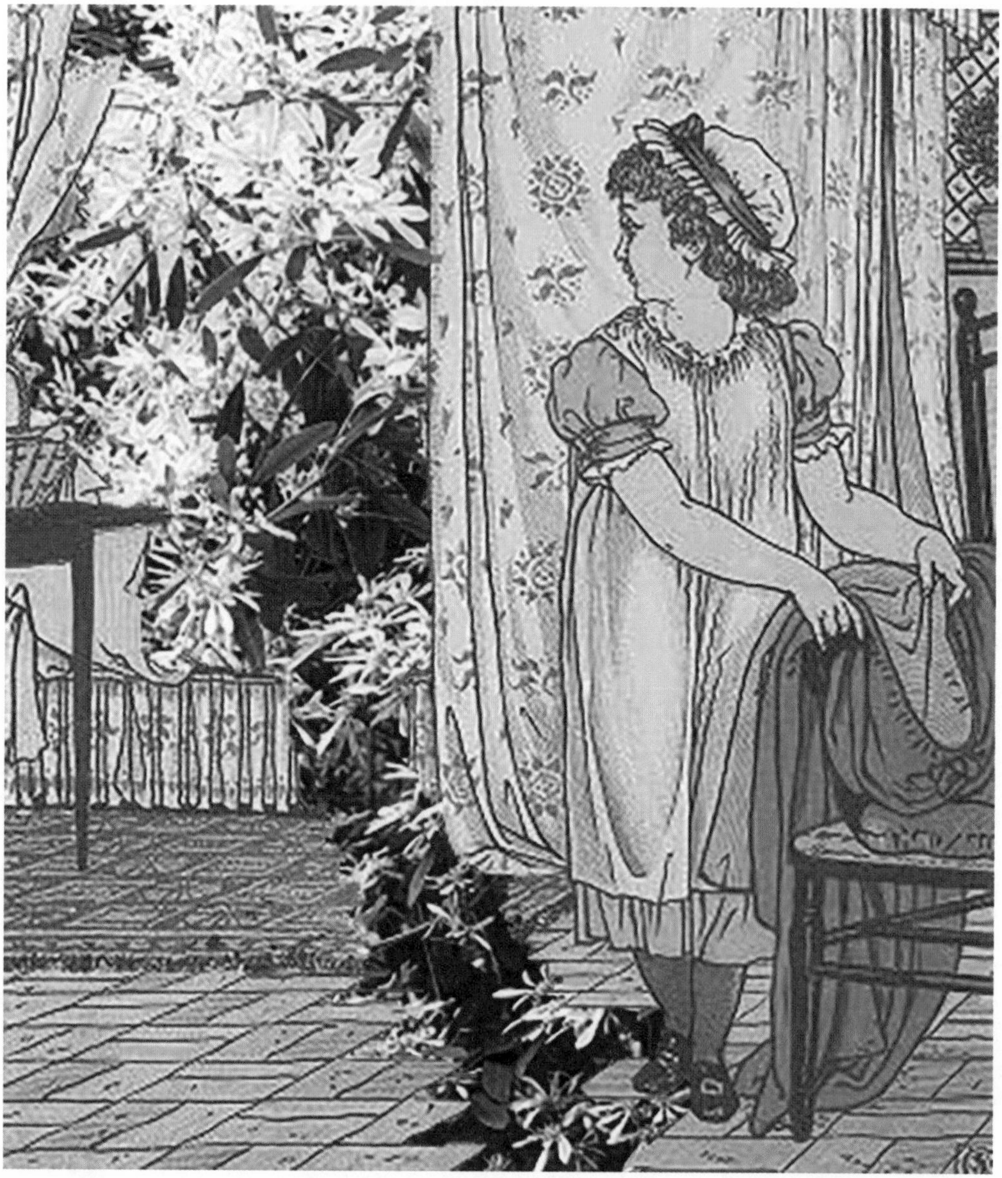

Little Red Hat: An Intermission

after Christian Schneller

Once there was a
Little Red Hat set

out for an ogre,

but on the way
her heart desired.

Red Walks Outside and Takes Into Account the Trees Before the Flowers

At the market, she would buy more rice. She would flirt with a bargain. She would disappear an egg through a narrow sleeve. In purple light and in under an hour, she would arrive to a smile that she shouldn't trust. She would measure the meat with her pulse. But at this moment, she feels like a stone and has set down her basket to brush a piece of hair undoing its proper course. And very soon, she will lift her tongue like a root-bed to clear her throat before moving towards dead-red sky.

Red Encounters a Stray Bullet at the Marketplace

At the market, something new hums. Time is a patient tender, of which she has too little. She works among crowds like a spool. An edge of a pound, a stray fruit and flower. The meanest haggle crowns her here and here. But *there*—an unaccustomed furl. Something pleasant around the jaw, the ends of his teeth: an invitation. She locks eyes with a uniform that will give her away to the stars. She smiles, her heartbeat high in her red throat. What cannot end at the end of this story? [Everything] She knows the route by heart, but my, what a pretty flower.

A Sleep Like Smile

The next morning and the next morning and the next morning she encounters the uniform—it presses itself into her dark edge. She cannot not think of it. She is turning a corner, rounding the eggs, and he is there again like a pulse. She will be late for breakfast, but she accepts an invitation. They are making plans. [Tomorrow and tomorrow] He brushes the back of her palm with the uniform's edge as he turns. It is rougher than expected. When she arrives back home, she is missing the eggs. [A beating] All night long she sleeps on a bed of dogtooth violets. In the dream, they are rooting their way into the ends and bits of her hair.

A Wolf Promises Happiness, or Still Life as a Fruit Basket

Linh says his mouth smells like rotting flesh. Thin cigarettes hang from its ends. At night, the world is full of sky and erasure. Red accepts the hand that rests at the small of her back. We aren't here for a very long time, the wolf said. Red accepts this, too. [She won't] At daybreak, he is kneeling beside a paved road—asking. Something brief and bright accompanies her before sunset, like a smooth rock she's been considering in her pocket.

Inviting a Wolf into Her Father's Bed

He was a trusting man, but not a stupid one. The wolf slept in ông ngoại's bed that night to ensure no snare for Red, no nonsense. Oh reader, must we simply explain everything? Must we know it all? [They were in love.] Their way was obvious. Ours is not.

Red as Brief Ecstasy

The routine was that it wasn't. Red climbed up into expanding bushels of flowers each new day; they were so bright she could barely see her own hands. The thought of a new life (a good life). The thought away from her mother's womb that was always busy birthing another impression. Maybe this would be a clean path, she thought. And delighted. [She encountered herself] Maybe this wasn't the way home.

Linh Delivers a Whisper, or Birds Never Undo their Own Nests

Linh didn't mean harm, but she did undo the basket. Said she saw. Said she heard. Said she knew a thing. Was she mistaken? [She was, but not wrong] More and more men wore uniforms; she couldn't know for sure. Said she could show her herself. Said she could prove it any given afternoon.

Why Are You So Sad, Red?

To get there they had to drive through the woods by motorbike. Linh said she knew where he lived most. It took half of the rays and countless flowers and she said she would prefer to see the specter by herself. She knocked and held her breath. Exhale on a familiar face that still smiled when the clothes slipped. Inhale in a silhouette of a round form behind him. A baby above and below her arms. Pretty, Red thought. *Who is it? Invite her in.* Red passed a hand over her eyes and became a hole. She dismissed the wolf who would later beseech a stone, lose ten of his years to a prison camp, and send letters across the sea season after season. [She still read them, kept them] She dismissed Linh who knew she'd done a good and vicious thing. Back inside the woods, she made a home in nests and shells. She tended the water, she grew hardened hooves. If she couldn't become a new dawn, she'd settle for a buffalo. Sweet shadow singing to herself, responsible only to the grass and its tough love, hard work, circumstance, circumstance, cruelty, more laughter, and to no one, no one here by that name.

Hungry Poem in the Language of the Wolf

Call us what you will // thief, slut, mastermind, reaper, ordinary time

calls us mis-memory, we were born // in a time of great need,

wanted nothing that wouldn't pay us // when my mother is

sick when I am sick, we spend it *talking talking* // my ear pressed

up into a dim receiver // language melting brain off my lips // most

petty scintilla could be more concise: she said too much,

wanted too little, wasted too much time //

And when I sat her down and said *speak, I'll listen* // when I

sat her down and asked about forgiveness, I found a mangle

// found deluge, a roster of dead infant brothers, and a

pattern, my pattern, my sister's pattern, or

curricula on how to fail at near-nothing except suicide

// but forgiveness? No, there isn't room for that kind of grief

// out here on laughter's buoy, out here //

where all the women in my line know the woods before their beds

// where memory's selections rhyme with survival's pitted, stony lake

// and death here is something you joke about, flirt about,

provide encasement (don the frill, don the grandmother's hat) // and you take

the next stupid little girl out // quick // before she wants something

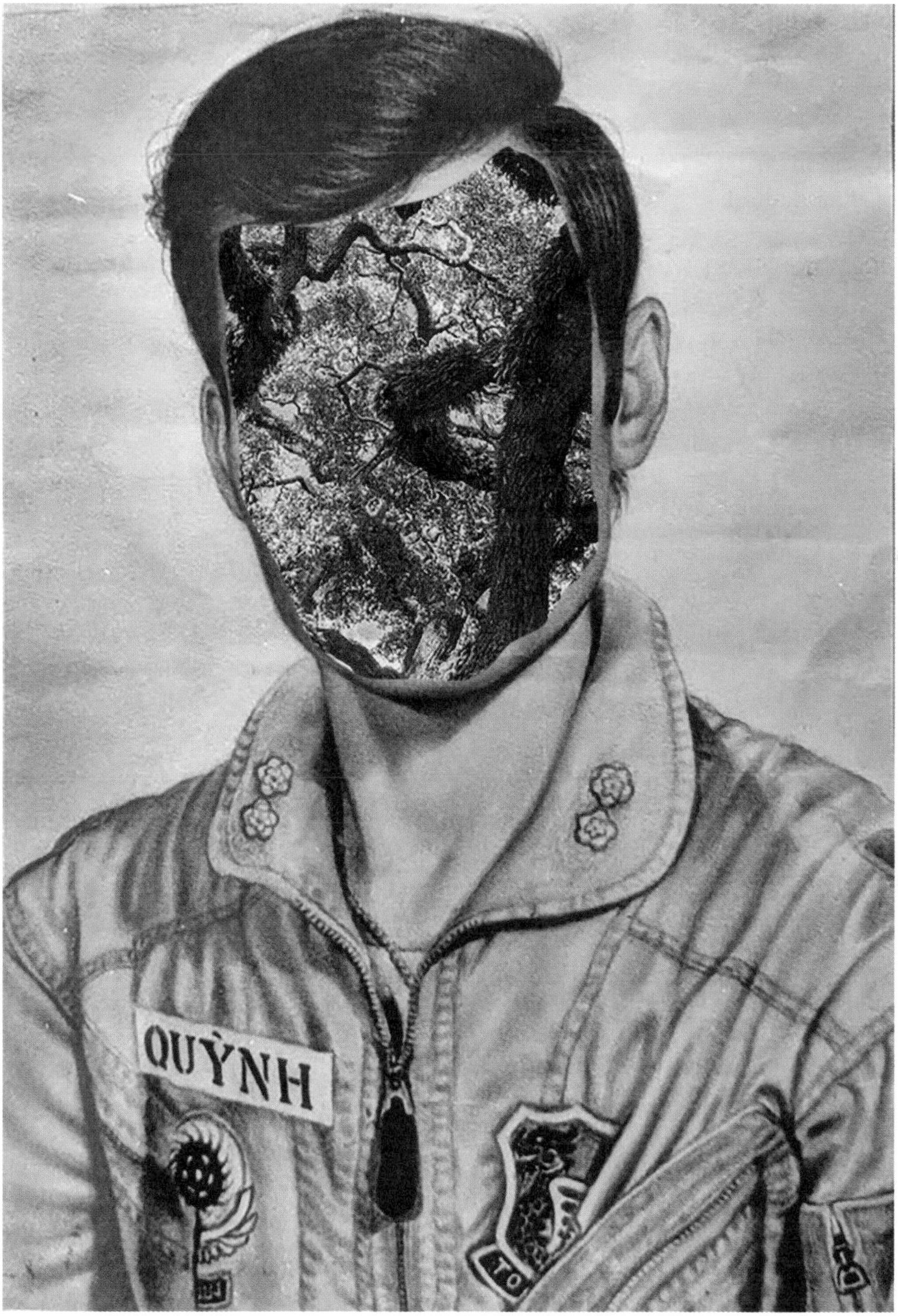
QUỲNH

Little Red Hood

after A.H. Wratislaw

Once upon a time
a darling damsel

said I WILL OBSERVE

THE LATCH and with
that, everything

looked so strange.

Oh, how frightened
I have been; it was so

dark in the wolf's maw.

THREE

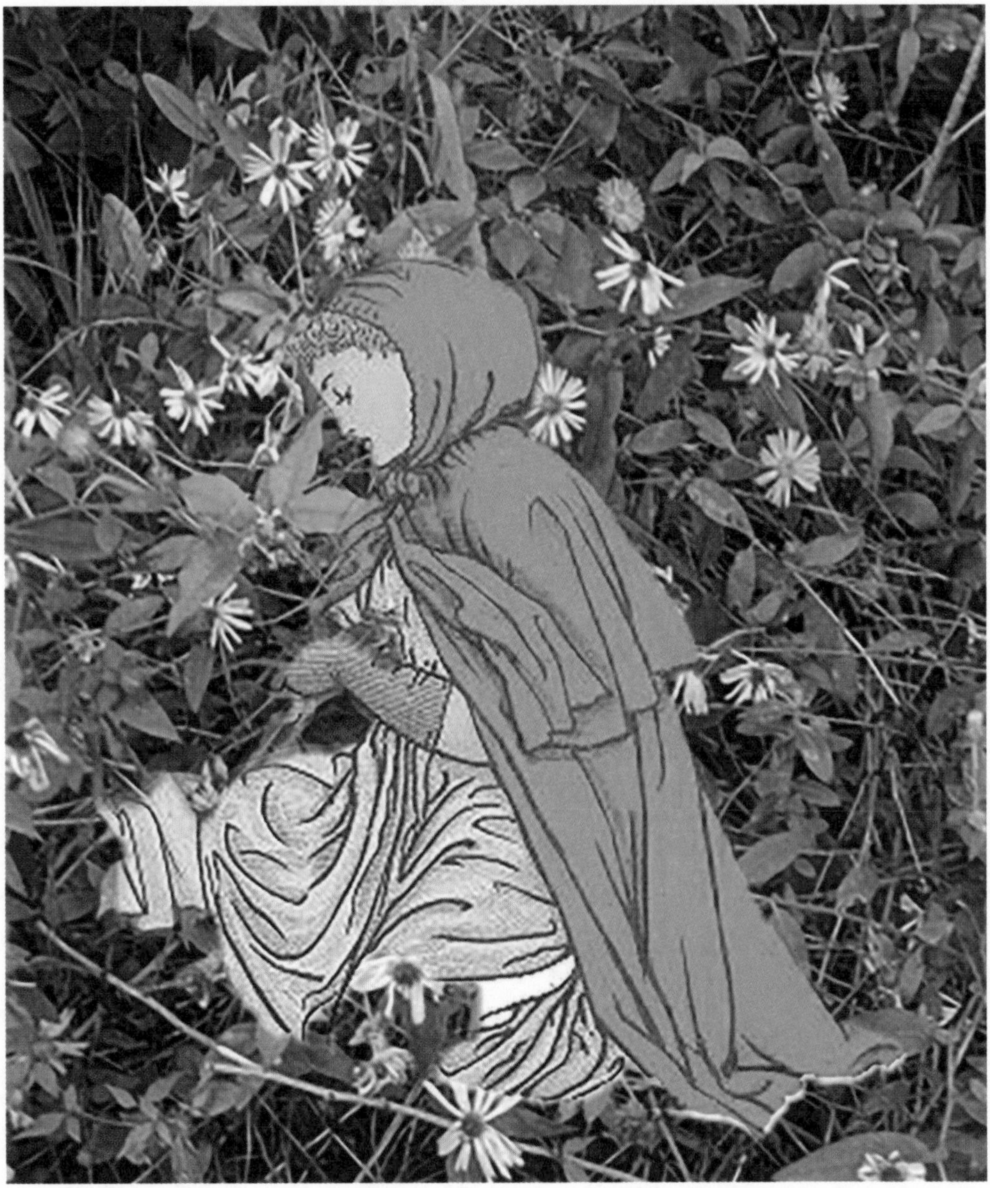

Little Red Cap

after Jacob and Wilhelm Grimm

Once upon a
grandmother who did

not know what to give
the child

a little cap of red velvet
a piece of cake
a bottle of wine

Here is a mind for your
manners, or nothing

in the woods. She did

not know a wicked animal,
you must not know this place.

Sunlight breaking through
the trees, very pleased

The wolf pressed the latch,
her clothes, got into

bed with a big mouth.

A huntsman

passing by, snoring loudly.

An old woman, snoring loudly.

Little Red Cap
ate the cake,
drank the wine,

told the wolf
EAT ME UP

and did not
open the door.

Kleptomania, 1991

We were masters of vanishing:

a five-ring troupe of

doves with purposeful hands.

One for the candies, one for

the wallet taken behind the

bleachers at the skate rink.

One for the Vienna sausages

for snack, one for the watch

to please a new friend.

Stealing is an art that's easy

to master. A quick scan of

camera placement, and the

patient breeding of panic with

nonchalance. What cannot

begin at the ends of our fingers?

What wild notion of crime

will hold them still?

Kleptomania, 1993

Or the fact that I cannot

talk about stealing

without mentioning women

mostly do it or at least

are more punishable for the

crime of taking what's

not rightfully theirs. On the

other side of the world, you learn

how to haggle. A skill that's

lost on price tags and door

alarms, standing tight-

lipped at each entrance. No

nonsense. On Fridays, we

lined our purses at the

buffet and returned home,

each door unlocking for

our bounty of squared pizza

and tiny muffins.

What bright laughter

filled our pockets, quietly

taking against the cruelty of

parking meters and waged time.

The secret of breadsticks passing

under the table made them

ours over cartoons, over tea

before bedtime, over

newspapers with water and

milk at dawn. Until we were full

up with it—the notion

that the world was ours, would

always be ours if you could

flex a wrist in the dark.

If you knew how to meet a

stranger's eye with a smile

like a private, sealed lock.

Kleptomania, 2023

Two decades later, my oldest sister

still worries about the photographs

taken in the grocery store breakroom.

The way the sweaty man's eyes scanned

my mother's body and told her she was

lucky—that we were all very lucky girls.

In another version we are

wrist-punching the man's glasses and

running for the door, we are

flinging open cash registers and

redistributing nametags. We are slicing

deli meat rapidly behind the counter

for our lunch. We are not standing

under fluorescence, choosing

whether to smile for the evidence

of our wanting too much at a time.

Kleptomania, 1992

And how to know when you've

taken too much? Once I shoved

a handmade placard down

the front of my pants at a

stripmall and felt nothing.

When they caught us, my friend

was a silent beacon even though

I was the one ruled an accomplice.

Hips grinding against the wood

of a trained deed. I admit I was

scared when my mother

arrived despite my calm

hoof. What happened

next probably isn't in any

child-rearing manuals or

other kinds of dictionaries. At my

periphery, a wild animal leapt

from tall brush lining the gas station

straight into traffic.

After a reign of expletives, we

left the deep woods. We plucked

violets unrepentantly from

neighbors' lawns. We

dashed around tidy rows all

evening like someone had just let us out,

like nobody could ever own

a single thing.

Little Red Riding Hood

after Thomas Nelson & Sons

A girl who lived ages ago

was made of red cloth,

conversation, and an errand.

  Not far a wolf talked so
politely, he made her forget.

     Pain undressed quickly,

trembling open—

and in rushed all that had passed:

the bloodthirsty slew

and red life at last.

Buffalo Girl

for my mother and Triệu Thị Trinh

History makes little bundles out
of the unthinkable

young boys carve

      three-foot breasts

to keep your story otherworldly and
      ridiculous; a crisp blade slips

from view   We stand

at the Albertson's Customer
      Service   and I hold my

breath   as you ready a

    well-worn   trap
      discount oversight ::

        grave mistake

A set of eyes

      exhaust   and I

    almost feel   for
our opposing force   who does not

know the   survival of   ants

      under glass ::

long after   your death you haunted
soldiers' dreams   the Chinese

Commander that slayed you built

                fallacies to   try and keep you
                                                                still
Poor men   and their

        fantasies of time and   blood

that pass only during the duration   of war

Victory   painted   the
parking lot   lucky-red

In every   windshield   I swear   I saw
the   glint of   slow storm

        in your eyes

History books are forever

        missing the details   of unfathomable

loss—   providing   discounts
    on   over-stocked goods   *You are my*

mother   —minor   warrior—   who has

        never needed   saving   who has
        never needed   memory   to make

a home   (a good home) alone

                            in the   woods

Catalogue of Random Acts of Violence

Where are you from?
Where is your mother from?
But can you speak it?
Can she speak it?
How long has she been speaking it?
Are you better at reading or speaking it?
Do you have family there?
Do you think you look like her?
Where are they?
And where are they now?
Do people tell you you look like her?
Can you understand her?
Can she understand me?
How much Vietnamese is he?
Who do you think he looks like?
Do you have another name?
Can you cook it?
When did she?
Why didn't she?
Why can?
Why cannot?

In Earnest, She Replied:

The Woods
The Woods
The Woods
The Woods
The Woods
The Woods
The Woods
The Woods
The Woods
The Woods
The Woods
The Woods
The Woods
The Woods
The Woods
The Woods
The Woods
The Woods
The Woods
The Woods
The Woods

The Woods

Name mame   mama
mama maim name

mama   mama

O O O if you knew how much

woods I own how much now
woods I know you might

turn straight into stone—
astounded, your face

like love folding me back down

into a bed of incomplete flowers

The Grandmother

after Achille Millien

Taking needles
to the house

that killed her,

the little girl
put a bottle of

blood on the shelf.

Her flesh
in the pantry.

Her bodice, her dress,

her petticoat, and her stockings into

the fire.

BETTER TO KEEP
MYSELF WARM

WITH THE OUTSIDE.

The grandmother
turned
away

from the door.

In the yard, a red

plum tree stood.

Poem in Which I Narrowly Escape My Birth

Do you ever feel like flesh? I do.

Bleached poem about the

broken jade bracelet my
mom hid in the front of

her underpants on a

helicopter for which
she bartered a broken fairy

tale. USA #1 on the   skip
track, skipping here we go 'round

the mulberry bush babe—   stick
it around your fat, white

wrists until it cracks. Bright-
light-waisted fingers, the

same size, but it's all different
now, she said,   *it's all gone.*

Smoothed down panic
with a memory

never there to
begin with :: some clean

country of arrivals and plenitude,
some fluent daughter's   mouth

to place seedlings and
transpiration.

And the story about the dead-
faced sergeant doesn't need

translation.   Hell, it doesn't
even need words :: Mama:

know a traveling girl with
a basket never keeps the

bread or the wine. She

loses talons for a time and
forgets the image of her

grandmother's face.

Keep it on your   person,

keep it   forever   under

gauze, keep it   safe in the
brick of wet   banana leaf-

loss, find me, gone   too,
for   you.

Somewhere   between
the dead sergeant's   deed

and the   sea.

Madame Nhu's Áo Dài, 1946

for Trần Lệ Xuân

Before the fit trim and the clapping
      of hands: a face bent in

violent repose. Still, the photograph
      of a captured figure with a

blanket for a shield and a baby
      on a battlefield.

This is not where we die and later,
      she would deny an interview

after the age of fifty-two. The projected image
      is no match for time's continuous

undoings: crossroad cruelties
      etched under lash. A

student of the Lycée Albert Sarraut, Madame
      Nhu was fluent in protection,

utility, and beauty's arsenal, but the civilizing
      mission had one message:

to burn the piano that held no secrets,
      to cast the face away like stone. In

her prime, she spoke French at home
      and could not write in

her native tongue—sharp thorns
      catching fabric, aflame.

There is a tradition of noble and heroic
        mothers here. After all,

Lê Lợi hid from the Chinese under
        his mother's skirts. Buffalo

Girls know how to tie a permanent
        knot around incidence, how to

mine mythology's antidotes for the
        fate of carrying and burying.

Madame Nhu was many things
        including a dancer, once a

soloist at the Hanoi National
        Theatre. She

        dragged hems

        across the knife's brink

between death and retreat. It is here
        where we depart (still alive)

        while inside, the Viet Minh are
steadying the flame, forgetting about

        the baby who—covered by
her mother's jacket—is turning

        away from the tidy story.

Is taking heaps of cloth into laughter,

        undoing each perfect edge.

Kleptomania, 1978: To Know and Laugh At the New Country

Hands spending, hands

undid and undoing a clock
with no hands that thumb

a way through hangers,
that switch the tags, that

strangers pockets, that reject
the terms of protection.

We cannot know what

you cannot hold and here,
for you: a perfect

peach in the palm of my
hand. Let it disappear

you. Have it hunger

across still-bent
bodies in

repose: one muddy
river to another.

And look: a wasp, the
taste of Big Macs and

nuclear-red Twizzlers—
our mouths savoring air.

Four firm wheels and

traffic lights, drive-thrus
and dirty dancing.

I said look:

it was worth it
for a time.

New World Ghost Story

Here lies the house
that she traded for blood,

that the siblings still
fight over—the domicile that

repels division.

Of course, it would be
filled with white

ghosts inside and white
ghosts outside, calling

about the white fence around the
way of telling you this is about

the time ông ngoại laughed
in the face of a ghost

that pressed nightly on his
chest, he was so full up

of it :: terror repeated long

enough becomes pure

comedy and what else can you
do but laugh and laugh

about the time the nuns on
bicycles shouted slurs

against the new neighbors,
taking. Or the time that

I wandered into the backyard
and finally knew a dead thing.

Or how ông ngoại, out of
nostalgia and spite,

snapped the neck
of the chicken he kept

right there on the front lawn
for our supper without

pause, luck unraveling
in his raspy hands.

On the sidewalk, a pair of

mistaken ghosts
mounted their bloodied bicycles,

mouthed   *oh*
                    oh
                        oh

and fled.

The Furies

That the Furies sprang forth from the blood of castration

That the confession didn't bring back the hometown

That departure never crossed out the stars

That the word *Erinyes* is of uncertain etymology

That most tragic things are

That the punisher(s) of the moral crime, infidelity, murder must bear the burdens

That Eurydice was never asked where she'd prefer to stay

That the woods obscure as much as they protect, that at least you can lay there

That there are so few public places to exhibit pain

That the image of the image of my mother in Vietnam is a birth certificate that
doesn't exist

That I don't know her in her mother tongue

That I don't know my mother's mother in any tongue

That this too means loss

That this too means woods

That I can't write about the war without my face

That my mother is always worried about her heart

That the violent General is decorated

That most powerful men are sexually perverse

That there's no accounting for punishment

That punishment isn't justice for deletion

That punishment could never be satisfactory, ejaculatory, a pretty show dog's head on a stake

That I'd put it in a book in order to blood-shot my own eyes, brass-studded scourge in my hands

Catalogue of Random Acts of Violence

A little latch sent me running

across the parking lot back

into the grocery to find my mother

among jarred salsas. They were strangers—

a couple—coaxing me into their car like

lines in a film without candy.

I knew it was wrong before

they asked, before my small body followed

them out of the store—ever-obedient calf—

before a hand tried to grab my skull and whacked

my cheek as I turned and fled. The spring of my youth

brought cities that pushed hungry appendages into

my back, holding me still on public transit, at an

outdoor concert, at a crowded bar that smelled like

dead frogs. In SOMA in San Francisco

I felt the sun on my face before another

stranger's violence punched it out of

the sky. Hulking, spitting. I saw him

coming and I did not change direction.

I braced myself and looked him in the eye

before he took a fist plainly to my temple.

Stole nothing, said nothing, saw no one.

Tender, I watched him walk away as

he swore at the clouds about beasts

crowding the flood. Even this morning

a decade later with a child of my own to slip,

I sat beside a suburban creekbed when a man's

dog's nails dug into my back's flesh from behind.

I eyed its owner who looked away and said *c'mon git*

in lieu of an apology, or any mortal word: another stony

finger extended from the deep woods.

Back in the grocery and out of breath, a pink flower

bloomed on my cheek. My mother turned to look at me—

a rarity when we shopped. Her look seemed

to say, *which kind?* With silence

I said, *neither.* An inheritance and

a curse feel the same at the pit

of your core. Every day we are rounding

corners, observing the rack of frozen meat.

Every day I am sticking to my route,

fleeing the scene of perpetual undoing,

carving space for a red

writhing thing at the end of the street,

at the end of my wrists—something

soft and still and holding.

Hungry Poem with Laughter Coming from an Unknown Source

She's still there the further you look back. I mean before the war,

and the wolves, and the other war, and the French, and her departure,

and even the Chinese—I mean *that* way back. And since I'm talking

about my mother, let's talk a hair-down, cat-eyed perfection, heels on a

borrowed Vespa kind of laughter—filling whole highways

with her eyeliner (another kind of laughter) and a deep belly

laugh at the thought of the Trưng Sisters ever jumping from

a single thing besides the time it takes my mother to flip the switch

on a boring conversation with a dick joke—*what did she say?*—

I mean keep up, I mean *that* far back—when Vietnam knew a world

could be best run by women and more women with still more laughter

charging the void—a still-life silt, a nitty-knot of a lump in the throat—

that sensation between choking and uncontrollable, heaving laughter

at the very thing that controls you and your body and your mother's body and

my sisters—my dear sisters—we always had laughter for our bodies that kept

planting deeper into the woods // *groundcover* // insert cut-scene, rescind the fairy tale: we all know there are no true villains—we're just a bunch of hungry animals.

I would jump with you, I would. I would give it all for you—laughter at

sundown, laughter at the feet crushing statuary, laughter until our very

last word on this dying Earth that just keeps turning and turning its

silhouette shadow figures slipping back into human skin at dawn.

Near-Death Experience

Like a huntsman, I

catalog my mother's near-
death experience.

It contains a river,
early-morning solitude,

her curious wandering
in a new village as a girl.

My grandfather, like all
flawed men, was a hero

in this story. She laughs
when she talks about

being purpled by the water,
by death's closeness that

pressed into her like
the image of a dead

smoker's lung.

We joke most about
ông ngoại pulling

mouth-to-mouth:

the earnestness
of recovering loss,

the mechanical nature
of our bodies—*jump-starting*.

She still can't swim and
I hate the smell

of cars to this day. That
day I wandered too far,

I remember pretending

my bike was a careful

automobile, taking
speedbumps like

lullaby, feeling the
ease of squeezed

breaks—how tender
and human our tools

can be, unlike

the stony nature of
memory sills

or what I hate most:

the dark cloak on
death's proximity

from that moment—

a little girl struck by
a moving vehicle

should be dead,
said I looked dead,

but I can't remember
what color of metal

hit my temple,

can't remember who
shouted what,

or even the fitting
of my collar

bone cast
a day later.

How can I be sure
we ever emerged

from the deep?

How the dark
imprints a tiny tattoo

in the shape of life's
physical humor. I talk

my mother into
visiting my new home

in Florida. I will
see her soon.

She will say

how much

closer death
is to her now. I have
plans. I will pick

her up in an automobile
that's painted red.

I will reserve a day
for regarding the

big, vast sea
near which

I've made my home.

My Mother Reads Me Little Red Riding Hood as a Young Girl

After the cat is sated and garaged, after the dishes drip on a rack,
after the locks snap, after a swept floor, after ironed shirts and ties,

after dinner separates into Tupperwared tiers, after the
big star dies again in the sky, after *Unsolved Mysteries* and

my sisters retreating through separate doors. Before I learned to
read, my mother sang nightly from books—the cadence of rising

tones charged careless English with music off the page.
I'd listen to her work her way through its drama: the

little girl's errors hitched to curiosity, her wandering hands, the
way the wolf and the girl had much more in common than not—

both hungry beasts seeking nutrition and love and beauty. Most of
my childhood was a wander, but I don't know when she turned wolf, what

finally set her off through the woods alone. Yet even as the Huntsman
draws closer for us, I can still see Red's tender slip. I've seen

my mother's walking route and the way she carried my own baby like
a precious parcel from another life. Affection curves even into

her cruelest forms: my head bashed into the car dashboard, the stolen wallets
behind the ice rink's bleachers, even the shadow beneath her eyes

when she talks about money or big tits or who today is not being grateful.
What are we, but small creatures avoiding new versions of violence?

After the wolf is dead, after the girl and the grandmother are dead, after the wine is drank, and the basket delivered. After the woods are gone, after the story

is lost or repurposed, after the conditions of departure and the language are both forgotten. And after my mother is gone, after my sisters are

gone, after I am good and gone, too, may there be some minor figure blooming at the edge of this dense treatment. May she also skip sounding out words

like *circumvent, wander, curtains.* Have her eat a belly-full of principles and stone. Have her gulp the whole house down, while it's still kicking.

The True History of Little Golden-Hood

after Charles Marelles

The story begins something
like a pleasant girl,

something of a witch.

The girl stops to talk
with a wolf—

woodcutters frisking
her like a good dog.

The little hood, invisible,
trying to find the door.

I KNOW WHAT I'LL DO,

amusing herself by watching
birds make their   nests.

The grandmother, without heart,
made her a good mother,

but she never kept her word.

In fine weather she may still be
seen in the color of the sun.

You must rise early.

Aubade with Buffalo Girls in Flight

Forget the nighttime,   forget the tumble
and scourge. I didn't come here   to sing silly songs. I was born into this day

a buffalo.   I will die one, too. Violence is my pelt, my light-fanged hoof.
When I was girl, I haunted men. Took them apart in my daybed

piece by piece, then went to microwave another burrito. We
aren't the worst   of each day, surely.

Don't paint this   love a tragedy. Mother, I owe you my face. I owe you an
uninterrupted life, which is to say,   I owe you nothing for

what I left out of this catalogue.   Still, I owe you for tender volume,
or the way I   never told you I cried after

driving you home to the   airport that year. Oh, final song of mercy, oh,
mercy me.   I watched you   disappear through

sliding glass, my car's reflection snapping the flutter   shut.
How one could be   vicious and still be

love, still be kind, but never still. A crownless human in this   rutted lake: the
trace of   this core that can't be fully excised by tongue, by cut, by mere

deletion. How after so long in the wolf's maw, we remember how to get home,
how to grasp each other's earthly hands as we flee towards the woods and the

hearth buried deep under the basket, the cloak, the fur. Against all odds, I think
we'll find it there as we do, each day,   the indifferent sun.

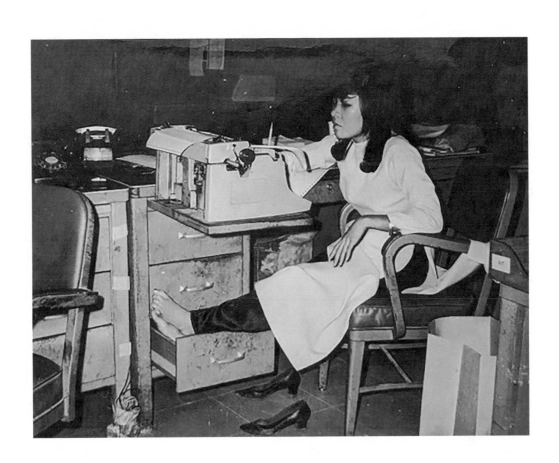

Appendix

"Little Red Riding Hood" or "Le Petit Chaperon rouge" by Charles Perrault, *Histoires ou Contes du temps passé* (*Fairy Tales from Past Times with Morals or Mother Goose Tales*), London, 1697

A mother sends her daughter to bring cakes to her grandmother. The little girl meets a wolf in the woods, and he tricks her into giving directions to her grandmother's house. He takes the shortcut. Faking the little girl's voice, he tricks the grandmother into telling him how to open the door's latch. He eats her. Tap, tap. Little Red Riding Hood arrives. The wolf hides under bedclothes and disguises his voice. He beckons her to come into the bed without her clothes. She remarks on his large legs, his ears, his eyes, and his teeth. He eats the little girl.

Moral: "Children, especially attractive, well-bred young ladies, should never talk to strangers, for if they should do so, they may well provide dinner for a wolf. I say "wolf," but there are various kinds of wolves. There are also those who are charming, quiet, polite, unassuming, complacent, and sweet, who pursue young women at home and in the streets. And unfortunately, it is these gentle wolves who are the most dangerous ones of all."

Little Red Riding Hood by B. Wilmsen, Triumph edition, pop-up book, Philadelphia, 1890.

A mother sends her young daughter to bring red wine and gingerbread to her ill grandmother at the edge of the woods. She warns her not to stray away from her course. Flowers distract the girl on the side of the path. She meets a wolf, and she tells him about her plans. He runs ahead of her to her grandmother's house while the girl delays among the flowers. He eats the grandmother and puts on her clothes. Little Red arrives and notices his large ears, his eyes, his hands, and his teeth. As Little Red draws near, the wolf grabs her, and she screams. A woodsman passing the cottage hears her and flings open the door, raises his gun, and shoots the wolf.

The woodsman guts the wolf but cannot revive the grandmother inside his body.

Moral: "Red Riding Hood learned on that summer's day, [t]he whole of the lesson "to obey": [a] lesson that all good children must know, [f]or there's always that wolf to tempt one so."

"Little Red Riding Hood" / "Little Red Cap" by the Brothers Grimm, *Kinder und Hausmäechen* (*Children's and Household Tales*), 1812, 1857, translated by D. L. Ashliman.

A little girl was sent by her mother to bring a piece of cake and a bottle of wine to her weak grandmother. The mother tells her to walk nicely and not to run in order to avoid breaking the bottle of wine. Little Red meets a wolf in the woods. She tells him the way to her grandmother's house, and he tells her to open her eyes to the flowers. She listens. While she picks flowers, the wolf travels straight to the grandmother's house. He lifts the latch, enters the house, and devours the grandmother. He puts on her clothes and draws the curtains. Little Red arrives and notices his ears, his eyes, his hands, and his mouth. "The better to eat you with." He devours the girl and falls asleep, sated. A passing huntsman hears the wolf snoring and remarks to himself that it does not sound like an old woman's snore. He uses a pair of scissors to cut the wolf's stomach while the wolf sleeps. The girl and the grandmother spring out of its belly, alive. They fill the wolf's belly with stones and when he awakens and tries to flee, he collapses from the weight of the stones and dies.

Moral: "Little Red Riding Hood thought to herself, as long as I live, I will never by myself leave the path, to run into the wood, when my mother has forbidden me to do so."

"The Tale of the Tiger-women" by Huang Chih-chun, *Guangyu chuxinzhi*, China (unclear province), 1803, translated by Victoria Cass and Gunter Lontzen.

In the Wan Mountains, there was a tiger that could transform herself into a human in order to harm people. In this area, a peasant sends his daughter to pick up a basket of ju-jube fruits and bring them to her grandmother. Her little brother accompanies her. In the woods, they meet an old woman. The old woman tricks them into thinking she is their grandmother and lures them back to her cave. At night, they fall asleep in the cave. The girl awakens to the sound of the tiger-woman eating her brother. Realizing her grave situation, the girl pretends she has to urinate outside. The tiger-woman ties the long gut of her brother to the girl's leg in order to thwart any attempt to escape. When outside, the girl removes the gut from her leg and climbs up a tree. A huntsman passes by and saves her from the tree. The tiger-woman later leads two other tigers to the tree where she thinks the girl is hiding. When they find her missing, the tigers become angry and devour the tiger-woman. It is unclear whether she was a tiger or a woman at the time of her death.

Moral: "He who wishes to harm others by means of fraud and deception is defeated himself in the end. But there must be someone meeting him who is not yet defeated. If a human being meets a creature who is both a tiger and an old woman, he should be careful."

"Little Red Hat" or "Das Rothhütchen," by Christian Schneller, *Märchen und Sagen aus Wälschtirol: Ein Beitrag zur deutschen Sagenkunde*, 1867, translated by D. L. Ashliman.

A grandmother working in the fields tells her granddaughter to come and bring her soup that night. Later, Little Red Hat sets out for her house. On the way, she meets an ogre. They go separate ways to the grandmother's house, but beautiful flowers distract the girl. Meanwhile the ogre kills and eats the grandmother. He ties the grandmother's gut onto the door and places her blood, teeth, and jaws in the kitchen cupboard. He climbs into bed in disguise just as the little girl arrives. The ogre tricks Little Red to touch, eat, and drink the bits of her grandmother. The girl takes off her clothes and gets into bed with the ogre. The girl notices his hair, his legs, his hands, his ears, and his mouth. "That comes from eating children!" And he swallowed her in one gulp.

"Little Red Hood" by A.H. Wratislaw, *Sixty Folk-Tales from Exclusively Slavonic Sources*, London, 1889.

A mother tells her daughter to bring a slice of cake and a bottle of wine to her sick grandmother that lives in the forest. She tells her daughter to be pretty and not to peep in all of her grandmother's corners. She tells her not to go out of the road. On the way, the girl meets a wolf. She is not afraid. She tells him the directions to her grandmother's house. He points out the pretty flowers to her and she runs deeper and deeper into the forest. The wolf travels straight to her grandmother's house and eats the grandmother. He dresses himself in her clothes and lays in her bed. When Red cannot carry any more flowers, she starts towards her grandmother's house. When she arrives, she notices the wolf's ears, eyes, hands, and mouth. The wolf springs out of bed and eats her up. He falls asleep, sated. A passing huntsman hears an unusual snore. "I'll just have a look to see what it is." He takes a knife to the wolf's maw and out jumps Little Red Hood. Out comes the grandmother next, barely alive. They fill the wolf's maw with stones and when the wolf awakens, he tries to jump, but the stones are so heavy that he falls and beats himself to death. Reader, I was confused too. The huntsman is pleased with the wolf's skin he acquired. The grandmother drinks the wine.

Moral: "As long as I live, I won't go out of the road into the forest, when mother has forbidden me."

Little Red Riding Hood by Thomas Nelson & Sons, London, 1894.

A mother sends her daughter to bring cheesecakes and butter to her ill grandmother. She tells her not to gossip or to talk to strangers along the way. In the woods, she meets a wolf, and he talks so politely, he makes her forget her vows. He points out the flowers to her. He goes along the straight path to her grandmother's house. While Little Red picks flowers for her grandmother, the wolf arrives at the grandmother's house and eats her. Red arrives and the wolf asks the girl to take off her clothes and quickly come into bed. She gets into bed and notices the wolf's ears, teeth, and eyes. "The better to see you! The better to bite!" In rush some passing men who have heard everything. They kill the wolf and save the girl.

"The Grandmother" by Achille Millien from Conte de la mère-grand, Nivernais, France, 1870, translated by D.L. Ashliman.

A mother tells her daughter to bring some fresh bread to her grandmother. At a crossing in the path, she meets a werewolf. He asks her whether she is taking the path of the needles or the pins. She says the needles. He takes the pins. The girl entertains herself by gathering needles. The werewolf arrives at the grandmother's house and kills her. He puts her flesh in the pantry and a bottle of her blood on the shelf. The girl arrives at the house and pushes open the door. A little cat in the house calls the girl a slut for eating her grandmother's flesh and drinking her blood. Reader, I was confused too. The werewolf asks her to get undressed and lay with him. He tells her to throw her bodice, her dress, her petticoat, her shoes, and her stockings into the fire. She does. When she climbs into bed, she notices his hair, his nails, his shoulders, his ears, his nose, and his mouth. "The better to eat you with, my child!" She tells him she must urinate outside. He asks her to do it in the bed, but she declines. He ties a woolen thread to her foot and lets her go. The girl ties the end of the thread to a plum tree in the yard outside and escapes back to her home.

"The True History of Little Golden-Hood" by Charles Marelles, *The Red Fairy Book*, 5th edition, New York, 1895.

A little peasant girl named Blanchette, more often called Golden-Hood (on account of her cloak of gold and fire), was instructed by her mother to bring a good piece of cake to her grandmother. Her mother tells her not to chatter with strangers along the way. Her grandmother lives in another village and the little girl travels through the woods to get there. She meets a wolf on the way. Woodcutters nearby inhibit the wolf from attacking her there in the woods. She tells him she is going to see her grandmother and tells him how to get there. The wolf takes a shortcut. Toc, toc. The grandmother isn't home. She is selling herbs in town. The wolf sneaks into the house and dons the grandmother's nightcap. Little Golden-Hood arrives and notices his voice at the door. She presses her finger on the latch and enters. He asks her to undress and lay upon the bed. She does, but she keeps on her hood. She notices his hairy arms, his big tongue, his mouthful of great white teeth. The wolf opens his jaws to swallow Blanchette, but she puts down her head crying, "Mama! Mama!" and the wolf catches her hood in his mouth instead. Her hood, her magical hood, causes the wolf pain. Like hot coals. The wolf, in pain, tries to find the door. At that moment, the grandmother returns from town with an empty sack on her shoulder. She opens her sack and the wolf springs headlong into the bag. The grandmother runs and dumps him into the well where he drowns. Blanchette eats the cake. Blanchette drinks the wine. Her mother scolds her, but Blanchette promises that she will never again stop to listen to a wolf. And she kept her word, as sure as the sun.

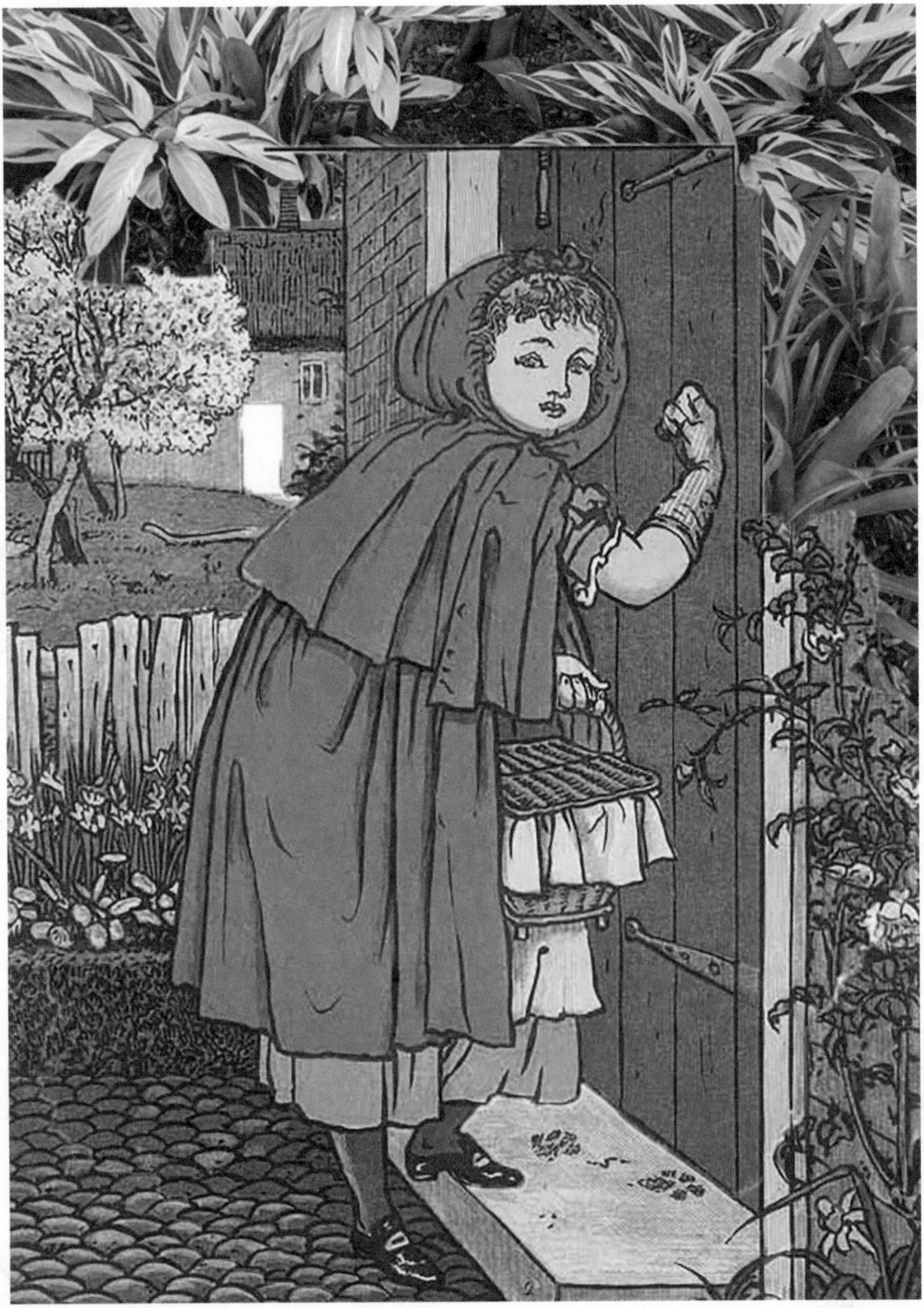

Notes

All "after" poems are liberal erasures of different versions of Little Red Riding Hood (see appendix for their synopses).

Little Red Riding Hood illustrations are erasures of Walter Crane's illustrations from Little Red Riding Hood, George Routledge & Sons, 1875.

Color photographs in collages were taken by the author in Treaty Oaks Park and the Arboretum in Jacksonville, Florida.

Black-and-white photographs belong to the author's mother, Kimle Mac Quick, and are used with permission.

"The Old Man in the Tree": the song lyrics at the end come from the song "Buffalo Gals," written and published as "Lubly Fan" in 1844 by the blackface minstrel John Hodges. The lyrics are a reference to sex workers who performed in bars, concert halls, and brothels in Buffalo, New York. The line "They danced by the light of the moon" appears later in Edward Lear's poem, "The Owl and the Pussycat" (1870).

"Ballad of the Red Wisteria:" the epigraph describes the cultivation of Chinese and Japanese Wisteria strains in the United States.

"Buffalo Girl:" this poem references Triệu Thị Trinh (Lady Triệu), a female warrior in third century Vietnam who resisted the Chinese state of Eastern Wu during its occupation of Vietnam. Her actual given name is unknown.

"Madame Nhu's Áo Dài, 1946:" this poem references Trần Lệ Xuân, one of Vietnam's most famous and most detested women from contemporary history. Suspected to have had an influential hand in the events leading up to the US war in Vietnam, she was also infamous for her glamorous, tight-fitting Vietnamese dresses, her vanity, and her cruelty.

"Hungry Poem with Laughter from an Unknown Source:" this poem references the Vietnamese Trưng Sisters (Trưng Trắc and Trưng Nhị) that led an armed civil uprising against Han forces in the south of Han China between 40 and 43 AD. It is rumored they killed themselves by jumping into the Hát Giang river when they were defeated, so as not to have to surrender to the Han.

Acknowledgments

Grateful acknowledgement to the editors of these journals where the following poems have previously appeared:

Best American Poetry: "Hungry Poem with Language Coming from an Unknown Source"

B O D Y: "My Mother Reads Me Little Red Riding Hood as a Young Girl";

The Boiler: "New World Ghost Story," "The One in Which the Wolf Wins", "Little Red Riding Hood";

Carolina Quarterly Anthology: "Madame Nhu's Áo Dài, 1946";

DUSIE: "Catalogue of Random Acts of Violence";

Hobart After Dark, reprinted in *Best American Poetry:* "Hungry Poem with Laughter Coming from an Unknown Source";

Hobart Pulp: "Ballad of the Red Wisteria";

The Seneca Review: "The Woods," "Catalogue of Random Acts of Violence" (originally as Catalogue of Random Acts of Violence II), "In Earnest, She Replied:," "The Tale of the Tiger-Women";

The Southeast Review: "Buffalo Girl," "Kleptomania, 1978: to Know and Laugh at the New Country" (originally as "Kleptomania V: To Know and Laugh at the New Country"), "Poem in Which I Narrowly Escape my Birth";

Triangle Poetry Twenty-Twenty-One: "Con Cào Cào";

Up the Staircase Quarterly: "Phylogenetics," "The Old Man in the Tree";

West Trestle Review: "The Stony Lake";

wildness: "Kleptomania, 2023" (originally as "Kleptomania III");

You Are the River: North Carolina Museum of Art Anthology: "The Wild Water Buffalo."

A short excerpt of this manuscript was published in *Carolina Quarterly* in Spring 2020. A digital, audio chapbook of a short excerpt of this manuscript was published under the title *RENDER* by the Eat Poems series in 2022.

My fullest gratitude to my mother, Kimle Mac Quick, who taught me survival through ferocious love, illogical manifestations of bravado, and a cantankerous suspicion of all forms of authority. Even when you're wrong, you're right, and even when you're gone, you're with me. You've always been the first poem. Deepest thanks as well to my fellow Buffalo Girls and my dear sisters: Judy, Jacki, and Jeanette. We made it through the woods alive, even though it always lives inside us. Thanks also to my father, Paul, who survived a household of five powerful women practically unscathed. You gave me my sense of humor and most importantly, disappearance magic, for better or for worse. Thanks also to my life partner and best friend, Daniel Stark, ever-graceful Libran whooping crane, who has always provided me a way out and a way back into my poems. Thank you to Annie and Evan for your love and for being rare models for a life of learning. Deepest gratitude to my son, Adrian, for being the lifeforce, the foil, the only path in everything I do.

Thank you to early readers, especially to Colin Dekeersgieter and Kylan Rice, whose podcast, *CQ Speaks* for *Carolina Quarterly,* and insightful conversation on a suite of poems from an early version of *Buffalo Girl* in 2020 provided the catalyst for revising and seeing this manuscript to completion despite pandemic depressions. Your dedicated attention was a surprise and a gift and convinced me that readers, even strangers, would pick up the breadcrumbs. Thank you also to Han Vanderhart, Dorsey Craft, and Marianne Chan for reading full, early versions of this manuscript in one of my many fever dreams. Your invaluable feedback, your own poetry, and your encouragement were the buoys that sustained me throughout the process of developing this book.

All my love to the poets and friends in North Carolina as well as the new communities I've found here in Jacksonville, Florida, with special thanks to Keith Cartwright, Nick de Villiers, Laura Heffernan, Jenni Lieberman, Dorsey Craft, Anne Phister, Anna Claire Hodge, Carolyne Ali-Khan, and Mark Ari. You've made life materially and existentially possible here, even when everything felt on the brink of collapse.

My love also to my *AGNI* editorial family, especially to Jennifer Kwon Dobbs, Bill Pierce, and Rachel Mennies. A big shout out to my Honey Literary family as well for providing a truly safe space for certified Buffalo Girls.

Thank you to Aracelis Girmay, Peter Conners, and the entire BOA team for believing in this manuscript and for the inspiring work that you do. Thank you to Buffalo Girls Dorothy Chan, Marianne Chan, Su Hwang, and Hoa Nguyen for their kind reception of this book and friendship.

Finally, I'd like to extend gratitude to the caretakers of my young son for allowing me the time and space to finish this project and to start a new job in a new city while writing through an ongoing pandemic. Thank you to Sandy and Mary Jane at Broad Street Children's Cottage in Durham, North Carolina, as well as to Pierce, Jennifer, Nicole, and Michelle at Melrose Preschool in Jacksonville, Florida who have spent thousands of hours watching Adrian throughout the development of this book. Your work makes the life that I love possible. May we never forget that so many women make thriving in this world perpetually imaginable.

About the Author

Jessica Q. Stark is the author of two full-length poetry manuscripts as well as four poetry chapbooks, including her most recent *RENDER* (2022). Stark's first poetry manuscript, *The Liminal Parade*, was selected by Dorothea Lasky for the Double Take Grand Prize in 2016 and her full length poetry collection titled *Savage Pageant* was named one of the "Best Books of 2020" in *The Boston Globe* and in *Hyperallergic*. Her poetry has most recently appeared or is forthcoming in *Best American Poetry*, *Poetry Society of America, Pleiades, Carolina Quarterly, Poetry Daily, The Southeast Review*, *Verse Daily*, and *Tupelo Quarterly*. Stark is a California-native, mixed race Vietnamese American poet, editor, and educator that lives in Jacksonville, Florida. She holds a BA from UC Berkeley and dual MA Degrees in English Literature and Cultural Studies from Saint Louis University's Madrid Campus. She received her PhD in English from Duke University. She currently serves as a Poetry Editor for *AGNI* and the Hybrid Editor for *Honey Literary*.

BOA Editions, Ltd. American Poets Continuum Series

No. 31 *The Fuehrer Bunker: The Complete Cycle*
W. D. Snodgrass

No. 32 *For the Kingdom*
Anthony Piccione

No. 33 *The Quicken Tree*
Bill Knott

No. 34 *These Upraised Hands*
William B. Patrick

No. 35 *Crazy Horse in Stillness*
William Heyen

No. 36 *Quick, Now, Always*
Mark Irwin

No. 37 *I Have Tasted the Apple*
Mary Crow

No. 38 *The Terrible Stories*
Lucille Clifton

No. 39 *The Heat of Arrivals*
Ray Gonzalez

No. 40 *Jimmy & Rita*
Kim Addonizio

No. 41 *Green Ash, Red Maple, Black Gum*
Michael Waters

No. 42 *Against Distance*
Peter Makuck

No. 43 *The Night Path*
Laurie Kutchins

No. 44 *Radiography*
Bruce Bond

No. 45 *At My Ease: Uncollected Poems of the Fifties and Sixties*
David Ignatow

No. 46 *Trillium*
Richard Foerster

No. 47 *Fuel*
Naomi Shihab Nye

No. 48 *Gratitude*
Sam Hamill

No. 49 *Diana, Charles, & the Queen*
William Heyen

No. 50 *Plus Shipping*
Bob Hicok

No. 51 *Cabato Sentora*
Ray Gonzalez

No. 52 *We Didn't Come Here for This*
William B. Patrick

No. 53 *The Vandals*
Alan Michael Parker

No. 54 *To Get Here*
Wendy Mnookin

No. 55 *Living Is What I Wanted: Last Poems*
David Ignatow

No. 56 *Dusty Angel*
Michael Blumenthal

No. 57 *The Tiger Iris*
Joan Swift

No. 58 *White City*
Mark Irwin

No. 59 *Laugh at the End of the World: Collected Comic Poems 1969–1999*
Bill Knott

No. 60 *Blessing the Boats: New and Selected Poems: 1988–2000*
Lucille Clifton

No. 61 *Tell Me*
Kim Addonizio

No. 62 *Smoke*
Dorianne Laux

No. 63 *Parthenopi: New and Selected Poems*
Michael Waters

No. 64 *Rancho Notorious*
Richard Garcia

No. 65 *Jam*
Joe-Anne McLaughlin

No. 66 *A. Poulin, Jr. Selected Poems*
Edited, with an Introduction by Michael Waters

No. 67 *Small Gods of Grief*
Laure-Anne Bosselaar

No. 68 *Book of My Nights*
Li-Young Lee

No. 69 *Tulip Farms and Leper Colonies*
Charles Harper Webb

No. 70 *Double Going*
Richard Foerster

No. 71 *What He Took*
Wendy Mnookin

No. 72 *The Hawk Temple at Tierra Grande*
Ray Gonzalez

No. 73 *Mules of Love*
Ellen Bass

No. 74 *The Guests at the Gate*
Anthony Piccione

No. 75 *Dumb Luck*
Sam Hamill

No. 76 *Love Song with Motor Vehicles*
Alan Michael Parker

No. 77 *Life Watch*
Willis Barnstone

No. 78 *The Owner of the House: New Collected Poems 1940–2001*
Louis Simpson

No. 79 *Is*
Wayne Dodd

No. 80 *Late*
Cecilia Woloch

No. 81 *Precipitates*
Debra Kang Dean

No. 82 *The Orchard*
Brigit Pegeen Kelly

No. 83 *Bright Hunger*
Mark Irwin

No. 84 *Desire Lines: New and Selected Poems*
Lola Haskins

No. 85 *Curious Conduct*
Jeanne Marie Beaumont

No. 86 *Mercy*
Lucille Clifton

No. 87 *Model Homes*
Wayne Koestenbaum

No. 88 *Farewell to the Starlight in Whiskey*
Barton Sutter

No. 89 *Angels for the Burning*
David Mura

No. 90 *The Rooster's Wife*
Russell Edson

No. 91 *American Children*
Jim Simmerman

No. 92 *Postcards from the Interior*
Wyn Cooper

No. 93 *You & Yours*
Naomi Shihab Nye

No. 94 *Consideration of the Guitar: New and Selected Poems 1986–2005*
Ray Gonzalez

No. 95 *Off-Season in the Promised Land*
Peter Makuck

No. 96 *The Hoopoe's Crown*
Jacqueline Osherow

No. 97 *Not for Specialists: New and Selected Poems*
W. D. Snodgrass

No. 98 *Splendor*
Steve Kronen

No. 99 *Woman Crossing a Field*
Deena Linett

No. 100 *The Burning of Troy*
Richard Foerster

No. 101 *Darling Vulgarity*
Michael Waters

No. 102 *The Persistence of Objects*
Richard Garcia

No. 103 *Slope of the Child Everlasting*
Laurie Kutchins

No. 104 *Broken Hallelujahs*
Sean Thomas Dougherty

No. 105 *Peeping Tom's Cabin: Comic Verse 1928–2008*
X. J. Kennedy

No. 106 *Disclamor*
G.C. Waldrep

No. 107 *Encouragement for a Man Falling to His Death*
Christopher Kennedy

No. 108 *Sleeping with Houdini*
Nin Andrews

No. 109 *Nomina*
Karen Volkman

No. 110 *The Fortieth Day*
Kazim Ali

No. 111 *Elephants & Butterflies*
Alan Michael Parker

No. 112 *Voices*
Lucille Clifton

No. 113 *The Moon Makes Its Own Plea*
Wendy Mnookin

No. 114 *The Heaven-Sent Leaf*
Katy Lederer

No. 115 *Struggling Times*
Louis Simpson

No. 116 *And*
Michael Blumenthal

No. 117 *Carpathia*
Cecilia Woloch

No. 118 *Seasons of Lotus, Seasons of Bone*
Matthew Shenoda

No. 119 *Sharp Stars*
Sharon Bryan

No. 120 *Cool Auditor*
Ray Gonzalez

No. 121 *Long Lens: New and Selected Poems*
Peter Makuck

No. 122 *Chaos Is the New Calm*
Wyn Cooper

No. 123 *Diwata*
Barbara Jane Reyes

No. 124 *Burning of the Three Fires*
Jeanne Marie Beaumont

No. 125 *Sasha Sings the Laundry on the Line*
Sean Thomas Dougherty

No. 126 *Your Father on the Train of Ghosts*
G.C. Waldrep and John Gallaher

No. 127 *Ennui Prophet*
Christopher Kennedy

No. 128 *Transfer*
Naomi Shihab Nye

No. 129 *Gospel Night*
Michael Waters

No. 130 *The Hands of Strangers: Poems from the Nursing Home*
Janice N. Harrington

No. 131 *Kingdom Animalia*
Aracelis Girmay

No. 132 *True Faith*
Ira Sadoff

No. 133 *The Reindeer Camps and Other Poems*
Barton Sutter

No. 134 *The Collected Poems of Lucille Clifton: 1965–2010*

No. 135 *To Keep Love Blurry*
Craig Morgan Teicher

No. 136 *Theophobia*
Bruce Beasley

No. 137 *Refuge*
Adrie Kusserow

No. 138 *The Book of Goodbyes*
Jillian Weise

No. 139 *Birth Marks*
Jim Daniels

No. 140 *No Need of Sympathy*
Fleda Brown

No. 141 *There's a Box in the Garage You Can Beat with a Stick*
Michael Teig

No. 142 *The Keys to the Jail*
Keetje Kuipers

No. 143 *All You Ask for Is Longing: New and Selected Poems 1994–2014*
Sean Thomas Dougherty

No. 144 *Copia*
Erika Meitner

No. 145 *The Chair: Prose Poems*
Richard Garcia

No. 146 *In a Landscape*
John Gallaher

No. 147 *Fanny Says*
Nickole Brown

No. 148 *Why God Is a Woman*
Nin Andrews

No. 149 *Testament*
G.C. Waldrep

No. 150 *I'm No Longer Troubled by the Extravagance*
Rick Bursky

No. 151 *Antidote for Night*
Marsha de la O

No. 152 *Beautiful Wall*
Ray Gonzalez

No. 153 *the black maria*
Aracelis Girmay

No. 154 *Celestial Joyride*
Michael Waters

No. 155 *Whereso*
Karen Volkman

No. 156 *The Day's Last Light Reddens the Leaves of the Copper Beech*
Stephen Dobyns

No. 157 *The End of Pink*
Kathryn Nuernberger

No. 158 *Mandatory Evacuation*
Peter Makuck

No. 159 *Primitive: The Art and Life of Horace H. Pippin*
Janice N. Harrington

No. 160 *The Trembling Answers*
Craig Morgan Teicher

No. 161 *Bye-Bye Land*
Christian Barter

No. 162 *Sky Country*
Christine Kitano

No. 163 *All Soul Parts Returned*
Bruce Beasley

No. 164 *The Smoke of Horses*
Charles Rafferty

No. 165 *The Second O of Sorrow*
Sean Thomas Dougherty
No. 166 *Holy Moly Carry Me*
Erika Meitner
No. 167 *Clues from the Animal Kingdom*
Christopher Kennedy
No. 168 *Dresses from the Old Country*
Laura Read
No. 169 *In Country*
Hugh Martin
No. 170 *The Tiny Journalist*
Naomi Shihab Nye
No. 171 *All Its Charms*
Keetje Kuipers
No. 172 *Night Angler*
Geffrey Davis
No. 173 *The Human Half*
Deborah Brown
No. 174 *Cyborg Detective*
Jillian Weise
No. 175 *On the Shores of Welcome Home*
Bruce Weigl
No. 176 *Rue*
Kathryn Nuernberger
No. 177 *Let's Become a Ghost Story*
Rick Bursky
No. 178 *Year of the Dog*
Deborah Paredez
No. 179 *Brand New Spacesuit*
John Gallaher
No. 180 *How to Carry Water: Selected Poems of Lucille Clifton*
No. 181 *Caw*
Michael Waters
No. 182 *Letters to a Young Brown Girl*
Barbara Jane Reyes
No. 183 *Mother Country*
Elana Bell
No. 184 *Welcome to Sonnetville, New Jersey*
Craig Morgan Teicher
No. 185 *I Am Not Trying to Hide My Hungers from the World*
Kendra DeColo
No. 186 *The Naomi Letters*
Rachel Mennies
No. 187 *Tenderness*
Derrick Austin
No. 188 *Ceive*
B.K. Fischer
No. 189 *Diamonds*
Camille Guthrie
No. 190 *A Cluster of Noisy Planets*
Charles Rafferty
No. 191 *Useful Junk*
Erika Meitner
No. 192 *Field Notes from the Flood Zone*
Heather Sellers
No. 193 *A Season in Hell with Rimbaud*
Dustin Pearson
No. 194 *Your Emergency Contact Has Experienced an Emergency*
Chen Chen
No. 195 *A Tinderbox in Three Acts*
Cynthia Dewi-Oka
No. 196 *Little Mr. Prose Poem: Selected Poems of Russell Edson*
No. 197 *The Dug-Up Gun Museum*
Matt Donovan
No. 198 *Four in Hand*
Alicia Mountain
No. 199 *Buffalo Girl*
Jessica Q. Stark

Colophon

BOA Editions, Ltd., a not-for-profit publisher of poetry and other literary works, fosters readership and appreciation of contemporary literature. By identifying, cultivating, and publishing both new and established poets and selecting authors of unique literary talent, BOA brings high-quality literature to the public.

Support for this effort comes from the sale of its publications, grant funding, and private donations.

The publication of this book is made possible, in part, by the special support of the following individuals:

Anonymous
Blue Flower Arts, LLC
Angela Bonazinga & Catherine Lewis
Christopher C. Dahl
James Long Hale
Margaret B. Heminway
Grant Holcomb
Kathleen Holcombe
Nora A. Jones
Paul LaFerriere & Dorrie Parini, *in honor of Bill Waddell*
Jack & Gail Langerak
Barbara Lovenheim
Peter & Phyllis Makuck
Joe McEleveny
David Mooney
The Mountain Family, *in support of poets & poetry*
Nocon & Associates, a private wealth advisory practice of Ameriprise Financial Services LLC
Boo Poulin
John H. Schultz
William Waddell & Linda Rubel